CW00661840

Kaz Cooke &
Simon Weaselpantz

PENGUIN BOOKS

Penguin Books Australia Ltd
250 Camberwell Road,
Camberwell, Victoria 3124, Australia
Penguin Books Ltd
80 Strand, London WC2R 0RL, England
Penguin Putnam Inc.
375 Hudson Street, New York, New York 10014, USA
Penguin Books, a division of Pearson Canada
10 Alcorn Avenue, Toronto, Ontario, Canada, M4V 3B2
Penguin Books (NZ) Ltd
Cnr Rosedale and Airborne Roads, Albany, Auckland, New Zealand
Penguin Books (South Africa) (Pty) Ltd
24 Sturdee Avenue, Rosebank, Johannesburg 2196, South Africa
Penguin Books India (P) Ltd
11, Community Centre, Panchsheel Park, New Delhi 110 017, India

First published by Penguin Books Australia Ltd 1998

13 15 17 19 18 16 14

Illustrated by Kaz Cooke
Typeset in 10/13 Freeway Roman by Midland Typesetters, Maryborough, Victoria
Printed and bound in Australia by McPherson's Printing Group, Maryborough, Victoria

National Library of Australia
Cataloguing-in-Publication data:

Cooke, Kaz, 1962– .
The little book of crap.

ISBN 0 14 027679 3.

1. Affirmations – Humor. 2. Australian wit and humor.
I. Weaselpantz, Simon. II. Title.

A828.302

www.penguin.com.au

The Intro

Welcome to the follow-up to *The Little Book of Stress, The Little Book of Crap*. Culled from the thoughts of idiots and poncy wankers everywhere, these marvellous quotes and thoughts will not help you at all in your day-to-day life. No, they are simply crap, compiled meticulously from the cream of the crap, worldwide. The book was written by the well-known craponagist and custard-wresting commentator Kaz Cooke and her colleague, the obscure medieval scholar and furry trout breeder, Simon Weaselpantz. As Shakespeare once said, 'I only ever read books smaller than my own codpiece'. Thank you, and enjoy.

Simon Weaselpantz

Be not estranged from your booty,
lest you need to shake it.

'The Devil Finds Work
for Idle Hands.'
In these Sad Times of
Economic Irrationalism he is
probably the only Governing
Authority with the Ability to
Manage it!

Hope knocks! Why were you down at the laundromat?

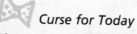 *Curse for Today*

May your Lust for life Wither and Waste within sight of the Vine of Veritable Voluptuaries!

It is better to give or receive
than never to have got a look-in
either way.

'All Comes to Him Who Waits.'
And Waits, and Waits, and
Waits, and Waits, and
Waits, and Waits,
and Waits.

Blessed are the lambs who get in
for their chop.

When the Middle Eye of the
Golden Buddha of the Trapezoid
Winks thrice, the Turbulence of
the Whirlpool within
shall Shift to Tumble dry!

Simon Weaselpantz

Dippy will do nicely for a while
but eventually you're going to
have to take a phone message,
or insure your own diamonds.

Curse for Today

May your descendants Maintain
the Great tradition of your
Ancestors by Continuing to
Stand Behind the proverbial
Door when the Brainy Bits are
Handed Out!

Speak softly and carry a large beef jerky.

– Davo Davidson

Wilt not in the Desert of Fiscal
Uncertainties: do a night course,
Become a Super fund manager
and Abscond to Majorca
with the Cash!

A lewd cuckoo gathers no moss.

Savour the Simple things in Life,
Like paper clips
and staple removers,
So when the Really Dull
things in Life Come along
They'll seem Exciting!

O the fruit doth not fall
so far from the tree!
Why then does one so often step in it?

If a-strolling in an Andean Clime,
Always carry about One's
person a Frilly Hanky:
You'll most Assuredly
Befriend the crafty Llama!

Be cautious in your life.
Is your office bugged?
Are you, yourself, a bit of a bugger?

Blessing for Today

May the Green marsupial of
Jealousy dull its Claws
in the Sclerophyll canopy of the
Great Southland of your Soul!

If you haven't got anything nice
to say, get yourself a publisher.

As Long as You're standing
Behind a safety Net,
a solid Concrete wall, and don't
smell like a Rotting Carcass,
it should be Perfectly fine to
Smile at a Crocodile!

Be kind and not querulous.
Do not gossip. Move quietly and
with dignity and speak only of
righteous matters. You shall
soon find that you have
some peace and quiet on your own.

Curse for Today

May the Love of Your Life
Be born in Another Age!

Blessed are those who see
beauty in all things around them,
for they have never been
to Tennant Creek.

When entering the Hallowed
Portals of The Crystal Temple of
the Galaxies, remember to Keep
your Aura within easy Reach
and Ensconce your Credit Card
in Your Y-fronts!

Time is meaningless and endless
and timeless. It matters not,
it bendeth to the will, it dreams
and slows and loops.
Unless of course
you have to be somewhere.

'The Meek Shall
Inherit the Earth.'
The Meek are doing Well,
the Earth's doing Fine, too,
and Piggies are Flying
Past your Window!

Glory to the New-Born King –
Now there's a pretty funny thing!
What a pity he wasn't a girl,
With three wise women called
    Pam, Bev and Merle.

Curse for Today

May the Cursed Transom of Your
Undercarriage Bang Noisily
Against its Superstructure
Throughout the Duration of
Your Sojourn in Time and Space!

Do not turneth your back on the person who hath forsaken thou. Hand gestures are more readily interpreted.

Remember:
If a Fellow Discovereth
Mistletoe upon his Trilby,
'Tis Best to Simply
Ignore it!

A bad love affair is like a river in summer. Wet, shallow and meandering for no particular reason.

If Life is a Journey,
with a Beginning and Ending,
just like a Train trip,
then I'm all for Fare Evasion!

Our disadvantages can be
opportunities, and our problems
little cherry pies in high heels.
Especially if we've been
taking narcotics.

When Channelling Negative
energies Try not to Point them
at Anyone and never do so
During a Thunderstorm or while
Talking on the Telephone!

Blessed are those with the gift of tolerance, for when they finally do their block it can be very entertaining indeed.

The bouncy shall inherit the cocktail recipe book.

Decorum is important. But not
if it gets between you and
the food.

Does your Mind resemble
a bachelor's Apartment
after a New Year's Eve party?
Then it's Time to
Move Out!

In the beginning there was beef,
Now tofu.
Earlier there was politeness,
Now mofo.

Curse for Today

When the Cornucopia of plenty
Spills its Bounty into the
deserving Pockets of the Blessed,
May you be Light Years away,
Stranded in Another Galaxy!

People are like sausages: it's
what's under the skin that's
important. So poke them with
a fork periodically.

Hasten Not to follow the
Ways of Terrestrial Kind,
for Ignorance can Only be
illumed by the Blazing
Halogen Lamp of your
Inner Alien!

For every man who cries Oh no!
Oh no! Oh no, John, No! there
are those who cry anon: Stop
being Such a drama Queen you
Big fairy Ning-Nong!

Silence is golden but so is the
hair of a Baywatch actress.

Do not mock the fleeting muse!
It is preferable to
a floating mouse.

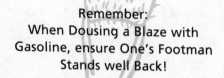

Remember:
When Dousing a Blaze with
Gasoline, ensure One's Footman
Stands well Back!

Virtue is its own re-run.

'He Who Laughs Last,
Laughs Best.'
Even if you feel like a Total
Dodo Being the Last person in
the Room to get the Joke!

The very first angel cried
hundreds of tears of happiness,
and each tear turned into
a golden orb and floated
into the air and turned into
another angel. Or there was
test-tube involvement.

Tired? Lonesome? Unhappy?
Need help and Guidance?
Please, just go Away and
Stop Pestering me!

Better a lone dinner of
dandelion weeds than
a sumptuous meal with
thine enemy. Unless you're
at all hungry.

Blessing for Today

When the silken Tresses of Stress
Wind their tenacious Tentacles
about your Person, May you find
the Hairbrush of Carelessness
on the Dressing-table of
Relaxed Abandon!

He that goeth about exultant
and boastful in thongs will
indulgeth a bull ant before long.

One should avoid Talking
to oneself. If one does, However,
Definitely don't Pay Attention,
and Never Answer Back!

Night follows day and day follows night and if you can't follow that nobody here can help you.

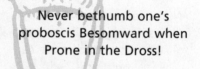

Never bethumb one's
proboscis Besomward when
Prone in the Dross!

What is Truth? Don't look at me.
People have been banging on
about it for centuries
and they still fire incendiary devices
at each other.

As you Stand Alone On the
Precipice of Despair Remember
this: you will have No One but
Everyone Else to Blame!

Couldst thou be a man whose
bosom burned with passion
and yet didst not set
the curtains afire?
No, I thought not.

Was the Colossus of Rhodes
really just the Ancient World's
Big Banana of Coffs Harbour?

Blessed are the peacemakers of the world, because sometimes it does seem as if there's only about three of them.

Blessing for Today

May the Handmaiden of
Spakfilla Lay Her Bounty upon
The Fiscal Fissures in the Temple
of Thine Piggy Bank!

The tree of life has many
branches, although sometimes it
can seem completely rooted.

Is the Search Engine of Carnal
Desire rummaging through the
Steamy Subconscious of your
Chat Line? Well Stop It and
Get back to Work!

There be those who can,
those who will, those who have,
and those who just
crap on and on about it.

The removalists Are in the Apartments of Calm Repose and they've dropped My Armchair of Inner Peace down the Lift Well of Harsh Reality!

Memories of sleep and sexual
high-jinks crowd mine bed –
not unlike this collection of
small children we've since had.

To stand Agape at a Sea-bear in
Accoupling Season simply
Invites the Besoaking of
one's Suitings!

Everybody is important, special, and worthy. Except people who you'd rather slap.

'Look Before you Leap!'
One should Always take
the Time to View the
Wonders of Nature!

Look ye to the thrifty grasshopper, thou sluttish sluggard, and change thy ways. What more reward could you want in life than eating insects and rubbing your legs together?

The Embezzler's cheque Bounces
and, having Bounced,
Moves On!

Up the airy mountain,
Down the rushy glen,
Bugger me if I can remember
What comes after then.

With apologies to
William Allingham, 1828–89

Blessing for Today
May the Roman Candle of Sweet
Redemption Light the highways
and Byways of the Hypermart
in your Suburb!

Art is whatever you're prepared
to pay for it to be.

Do you Dream in Gigabytes of
wondrous Pleasure Domes and
Horizons of boundless Delight,
only to Awaken in the
Shabby Bedsit of
Kilobytes' Remembrance?

Blessed are those who believe in
mermaids, fairies and the Easter Bunny,
for they are truly in need
of around-the-clock care,
whatever their age.

Never Attempt to board an
Omnibus if one is Deceased!

A pagan ceremony, full of fecund, whirling, oiled bodies and fundamental, rhythmically lustful drum beats cannot pave the way to heaven. But frankly, who cares?

'All the World Loves a Lover.'
However, when you split up you
suddenly Discover half the world
Secretly Hated almost
Everything about You!

Ah! Cry Freedome!
For all the Good it will do you,
You puir, hopeless Peasante!
Stick your breakefaste Turnip up
   Thine Arse!

Traditional song of the
manor house

Curse for Today

May the Wand of Unspeakable
Ugliness Continue to Smite
About the Bosom of Your Family
and Your Family's Families!

Favoured are those who put
others before themselves
because they are so much easier
to manipulate.

'We Aid You on Your Inner Journey, Without All-knowing Care and No Astral Responsiblity!'

From *The Handbook of Instant Wealth at the Font of True Enlightenment in a Free Market Economy*, by H. H. Baba 'Galosha' Weaselpantalama

It is far cheaper and just as rewarding to **pretend** you're utterly depraved.

All men look handsome in a
    tuxedo:
That is my mnemonic.
If you have had enough gin,
Easy on the tonic.

Better a fathead than a
bighead be.

Nothing can be Created Out of Nothing, So if you Are Nothing you will Always be Nothing! Ner! Ner! Nah!

People in glass houses should
change their underpants
in the dark.

'The Elephant Never Forgets.'
But when all is Said and Done
what does it Really have
to Remember?

Brave is the man who, when his limbs are smitten off, bites the platitude that feeds him.

When the Moon Barks and your
Quartz Medallion Howls and Jingles,
all is Simply Divine with
the Lunar Swoon Wrangler!

Do unto others as you would have them do unto you if they are the sort of person who also believes in this do-unto-others stuff and if not I wouldn't risk it if I were you.

Thought is lost in Action,
So join a Sporting Club and
Forget what you're Doing!

Ode to the Flu

Lift up thine eyes,
To the rays of sun,
And hopeth your head
Doth not fall orf.

The fleshy Husk of the Soul is the Carrying Case you're Lumbered with! You must Lug it down the Winding Footpath on the Wibbly Wobbly road to the Bus Stop for Eternity!

Masquerade is not the way to a man's heart: $50 000 might help.

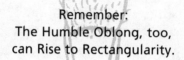

Remember:
The Humble Oblong, too,
can Rise to Rectangularity.

In thrall to the kingdom of envy, thou shalt never be content. But you might feel really very satisfied for a minute or two there, if you pull off a brilliant act of mean-spirited revenge.

Curse for Today

May the Secret Terror of your
Life be the Dark Knowledge
that you *Really are* A Hideously
Dull Bore!

The only way to true happiness
is to accept all that is put in
one's path with genuine joy and
as that is completely out of the
question it seems true happiness
is a crock.

When astride the Feral Pony of Stardust, racing the Sapphire Filaments Universal, equip your Personage with the Crop and Spurs of Holistic Discipline!

A simple life, a loaf of bread,
a pure heart, a train ticket,
a baby's sigh, a large parcel
of mining shares, a man
in a commissionaire's jacket
with no pants on.
All irrelevant to each other.

Blessing for Today

May the Dog-wolf of Desire
Clasp its Jaws upon the
Hindquarters of your Lust!

The wicked shall burn in hellfire
like a thousand pitchforks to
the private parts and all who
are non-believers shall
eternally shriek in agony.
Or there may be Bryan Adams
ballad involvement.

When rolling away the Stone
from the Tomb of Spiritual
Illusion, be sure to wear
Sensible Shoes!

A bad hair day:
ineluctable, in a convertible.

Always approach the Ruby Fire
of the Sacred Inner Flame
wearing the Asbestos Gloves of
Bitter Experience!

Knowledge is all very well, but rank stupidity is often rewarded surprisingly richly.

When you're down in the Dumps
you should Occupy your Mind,
So while you're down there
could you Look for that Itsy-Bitsy
Blue Thingummyjig with the
Yellow What-cha-ma-call-its that
I Accidentally threw out
last Tuesday?

You would do well to ensure
that the fairies have sent you
angel dust and not Angel Dust.

Time Was, when Time and Time
Again One Thought about the
Amount of Time Wasted
Thinking about Wasted Time.
Now one Doesn't have the Time!
Oh, my God! Is that the Time?

Meanness breedeth Resentment,
and the Hopeful
breedeth ostriches.

When making a Rod
for one's back, Always
Ensure that a Retailer of
Bepadded Jacketry
is within Hail!

In the endless scheme of things,
the waves rock to the sands, the
mountains roll to the plains,
the plains undulate to the
shore and the rabbit population
is partial to the hokey-cokey.

When being Strategically Redeployed by the Overlord in your Workplace, be Confident in the knowledge that the Millennium Bug will Utterly Destroy your former employer on the 1st of January 2000.

Heed not the jaw-juddering roar of a thousand would-be supermodels saying they eat like horses. (Sea horses, possibly.)

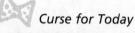

Curse for Today

May the earholes of your
Bank Manager be ever
Deafened to your
Persistent Pleadings!

It is better to dwell in a chookhouse than to be a slothful toilet cleaner.

If we meet in Another Life,
Please don't be Shirley MacLaine!

Alone, alone, alone.
Alone, alone, alone.
Alone, alone, alone.
Was it something you ate?

Remember:
The Circumference of your
Ambition is always
measured by the
Hypotenuse of
your Angle!

Happy dimplings maketh the picnic, tinkling laughter perfecteth it, but a horde of ants up your woozer is another thing entirely.

In a World where everyone
aspires to be Boundlessly Wealthy
Why not expire to Poverty –
Success is a Certainty!

As the wise virgins trim their lamps, so shall the foolish vicars forget about April First.

When swathed in the
Cloak of Dismay,
best not Seek Solace
in thy Gilded Snoutpiece!

Ignore your troubles and sing loudly, whatever happens. It goes down a treat with magistrates.

Fluorides and Toothpastes
Cannot fight plaque and decay.
Avoid eating altogether,
Keep your teeth, your figure
and Join your Ancestors!

Pride goeth before a bit of a stuff-up
and a filthy hangover
usually quick smart after that.

O Multipurpose Satanic One,
buggerise not the Utility Belt of
my Renovations Eternal!

Ode from a Dork

I sing of brooks, of blossoms,
   birds and bowers,
Of April, May, of June and July
   flowers.
I've even offered some of them
   loot,
But it hasn't got me a single root.

With apologies to
Robert Herrick, 1591–1674

Remember:
A fellow's Trousers are an
Essential item of Wardrobe.
Never forget to Disrobe
before having them Pressed!

You bear the seeds of your own destruction, but perhaps it is time to discuss fertilisers.

This Morning, One
Is like a Pop-up Toaster,
Hot, Sleek and Electrifying,
So Why do I *Feel* So Crummy?

Dost thou love and lose, wilt
thou? O watery depth of feeling
so dear to thy bosom. Fie!
Lest it doth begat the truthful
lips of thy majestic do stop me
if you've heard this one before.

May the Temple of Example Raine upon thy Sconce, the Everlasting Wrath of the Sentient Sartorial Style Master, flounced satin Pirate blouses, Indeed!

Man is by nature a political animal, with the emphasis on the latter and not so much on the former, especially when you consider how much the latter comes into it, frankly.

If through Misfortune at Table, one's doublet is Bedaubed with Bergylt, Console oneself with the memory of Dear Aunt Amelia's Unspeakable Accident!

It is folly to eschew wisdom,
unless you eschew it 100 times
before swallowing.

'There's No Rest for the Wicked.'
They're having Too Much Fun!

We doth remember what we strive to forget, and doth forget that which thee what we . . . where was I?

Blessing for Today

May the Kayak of Celestial Bliss
Glide gently to Rest in the Bed
of Spleenwort by your
Astral Window!

Taunt a physicist at a party with
the following handy phrase:
'Love makes the world go round.'
(The moon, by the way,
is made of cheese.)

Shoot for the Rapturous Stars,
Transcend earthly Woes
as a Born-again Astronaut,
launched on a Trajectory to
Utter Oblivion!

We have borrowed the future from our children. No wonder it looks so tatty and covered in spit marks.

It is not Sporting
to strap a Boiled Chicken to
the Leg of an Alligator Keeper
at Feeding Time!

Ode from a Drug Addict

Now the day is over, night is
    drawing nigh,
So I'm about to tell you another
    big fat lie.
Shadows of the evening steal
    across the sky,
Much in the same way as I have
stolen your CD collection, your
leather jacket and the phone bill
money . . .

With apologies to
S. Baring-Gould, 1834–1924

'A Rolling Stone
Gathers No Moss.'
But it sure as Heck wreaks
Havoc and Destruction, especially if
it's a rather Enormous Boulder!

All the wassailing in the poad
won't maketh the cracken bend
any fustier. Nay, and whoever
said that ought to be taken
down the back paddock
and shot.

If a Weasel befriends a Chap,
Well and Good; however,
Never let the Fellow Discover
one's Fiancée's Address!

Learn from the untrammelled soul of a puppy but there's really no need to poop inside.

Thy belly is like an heap of wheat set about like lilies. Look, it's in the Bible, it's a compliment. Don't flounce off, I only meant . . . oh forget it.

If at first you don't succeed,
throw a couple of tantrums.

Simon Weaselpantz

Blessing for Today

May the Laser Pen of
Technology's Bright Star
Guide your Finger on the
Road Map of the
Information Super Highway!